PASS IT ON
QUOTATIONS FOR ALL GENERATIONS

With Special Thanks To

These quotes have been passed on to me over time.
To the authors, contributors and original sources, my
thanks. To Steve Arrison, Chuck Robertson,
Twanette Clark, Greg Shira, Drew Harris, Heather Terrell,
Paul Johnson and Whitney Williams, thank you for your
ideas and support.

ISBN: 9666174-2-8

Printed in U.S.A.

PASS IT ON

Ordinary people accomplish
extraordinary things.

To my friend Frank Petrella
who passed away while I was in the process of
compiling this book – I'll always remember your words,
"The harder I work, the luckier I get."

Knowledge Is Power

Favorite quotes – we all have them – and if you're like me, these quotes help inspire you to turn your darkest days into days filled with an abundance of light.

I never planned to compile a book of quotes, until one day when I was reminded that quotes are meant to be passed on. From generation to generation, people from all backgrounds have coined phrases that are powerful and bold, yet simple and complete.

These are the ideals that leaders have passed on to their followers, that mothers and fathers

Shoot for the moon. Even if you miss it you will land among the stars.

– LES BROWN

Some men see things as they are and ask why. Others dream things that never were and ask why not.

– GEORGE BERNARD SHAW

The world is before us and we need not take it or leave it as it was when we came in.

– JAMES BALDWIN

I had a dream, which was not all a dream.

– LORD BRYON

Our willingness to create a new dream
or vision for ourselves is a statement
of belief in our own potential.

– DAVID MCNALLY

The grand essentials for happiness are:
something to do, something to love and
something to hope for.

– ALLAN K. CHALMERS

have passed on to their children and that we, as free spirits, continue to voice to those who are willing to listen.

A number of the quotes found in this book have been passed on to me and now I would like to pass them on to you. My hope is that you not only enjoy the quotes I have compiled, but also find wisdom in the true meaning of the words.

Remember – Pass It On!

–PAUL VITALE

Twenty years from now you will be more disappointed by the things you did not do than by the things you did. Sail away from the safe harbor. Catch the trade wind in your sails. Explore. Dream. Discover.

– MARK TWAIN

We will be known by the tracks we leave behind.

– DAKOTA PROVERB

We should quietly hear both sides.

– JOHANN WOLFGANG VON GOETHE

PASS IT ON

You can have anything you want if you want it desperately enough. You must want it with an inner exuberance that erupts through the skin and joins the energy that created the world.

– SHEILA GRAHAM

I speak ill of no one, and speak all the good I know of everybody.

– ANDREW JACKSON

If I'm dreaming, never let me wake. If I'm awake, never let me sleep.

– CHINESE PROVERB

Coming together is a beginning;
keeping together is a process;
working together is success.

– HENRY FORD

We are so very rich if we know just a
few people in a way in which we know
no other.

– CATHERINE BRAMWELL-BOOTHE

If you are going to be a bear, be a grizzly.

– JUSTIN SOLLARS

Pass It On

AND SO, MY FELLOW AMERICANS,

ASK NOT WHAT YOUR COUNTRY

CAN DO FOR YOU, ASK WHAT YOU

CAN DO FOR YOUR COUNTRY.

–JOHN F. KENNEDY

Every man of action has a strong dose of egoism, pride, hardness and cunning. But all those things will be regarded as high qualities if he can make them the means to achieve great ends.

– CHARLES DE GAULLE

The most beautiful thing we can experience is the mysterious. It is the source of all true art and science.

– ALBERT EINSTEIN

People don't just go to work to acquire, they go to work to become.

– DAN ZADRA

If you can imagine it, you can achieve it.
If you can dream it, you can become it.

– WILLIAM A. WARD

To create a vision, people have to get beyond their current inhibitions – they have to dream.

– JACK WELLS

We must use time creatively, and forever realize that the time is always right to do what is right.

– MARTIN LUTHER KING, JR.

We have always held to the hope, the belief, the conviction that there is a better life, a better world, beyond the horizon.

– FRANKLIN D. ROOSEVELT

Who never doubted, never half believed. Where doubt is, there truth is. It is her shadow.

– AMBROSE BIERCE

No one who ever gave his best ever regretted it.

– GEORGE HALAS

Pass It On

Life is no brief candle for me. It is a splendid torch which I have a hold of for only a moment, and I want to make it burn as brightly as possible before handing it on to future generations.

– GEORGE BERNARD SHAW

Do not follow where the path may lead. Go instead where there is no path, and leave a trail.

– RALPH WALDO EMERSON

It is not the size of a man but the size of his heart that matters.

– EVANDER HOLYFIELD

To every man there comes in his lifetime that special moment when he is figuratively tapped on the shoulder and offered that chance to do a very special thing, unique to him and fitted to his talents.

– WINSTON CHURCHILL

If you are doing your best, you will not have to worry about failure.

– ROBERT HILLYER

You can't stuff a great life into a small dream.

– H. JACKSON BROWN, JR.

Keep away from people who try to belittle your ambitions. Small people always do that, but the really great make you feel that you too can become great.

– MARK TWAIN

Living with purpose is more a question of what we put in than what we take out.

– HOWARD BARNES

People tend to resist that which is forced upon them. People tend to support that which they help to create.

– VINCE PFAFF

The height of great men reached and
kept were not attained by sudden flight,
but they, while their companions slept,
were toiling upward in the night.

– HENRY WADSWORTH LONGFELLOW

My message to you is: Be courageous!
Be as brave as your fathers before you.
Have faith! Go forward.

– THOMAS EDISON

The person with big dreams is more
powerful than one with all the facts. Never
give up on what you really want to do.

– LIFE'S INSTRUCTION BOOK

PASS IT ON

To love what you do and feel that it matters; how could anything be more fun?

– KATHERINE GRAHAM

Take a chance. All life is a chance. The man who goes furthest is generally the one who is willing to do and dare.

– DALE CARNEGIE

Hold fast to dreams, for if dreams die, life is like a broken winged bird that cannot fly.

– LANGSTON HUGHES

Great minds have purposes;
others have wishes.

– WASHINGTON IRVING

All men dream, but not equally. They who
dream by night in the dusty recesses of
their minds wake in the day to find that it
is vanity; but the dreamers of the day are
dangerous men, for they act their dreams
with open eyes, to make it possible.

– T.E. LAWRENCE

Give me a place to stand, and I will move
the earth.

– ARCHIMEDES

WE GROW GREAT BY DREAMS.

ALL BIG MEN ARE DREAMERS.

THEY SEE THINGS IN THE SOFT HAZE

OF A SPRING DAY OR IN THE RED FIRE

OF A LONG WINTER'S EVENING.

—WOODROW WILSON

The difference between the impossible and the possible lies in a man's determination.

– TOMMY LASORDA

When written in Chinese, the word crisis is composed of two characters. One represents danger and the other represents opportunity.

– JOHN F. KENNEDY

Before proceeding, one must reach out.

– WEST AFRICAN PROVERB

Pass It On

Each one of us contains the power to achieve greatness and you hold the key to your destiny.

— ALEXANDER LOCKHART

The world turns aside to let any man pass who knows where he is going.

— DAVID JORDAN

Putting off an easy thing makes it hard, and putting off a hard thing makes it impossible.

— GEORGE HORACE LORIMER

Let me win, but if I cannot win, let me be brave in the attempt.

– SPECIAL OLYMPICS MOTTO

The thing always happens that you really believe in; and the belief in a thing makes it happen.

– FRANK LLOYD WRIGHT

Faced with the choice between changing one's mind and proving that there is no need to do so, almost everybody gets busy on the proof.

– JOHN KENNETH GALBRAITH

He who has never failed somewhere;
that man cannot be great.

– HERMAN MELVILLE

Problems are the cutting edge that
distinguish between success and failure.
Problems create our courage and wisdom.

– SCOTT PECK

I would rather be a failure at something
I enjoy than be a success at something
I hate.

– GEORGE BURNS

Do not let what you cannot do interfere with what you can do.

– JOHN WOODEN

No man knows what he can do until he truly tries.

– PUBLIUS SYRUS

Change means movement. Movement means friction. Friction means heat – and heat is required for growth.

– DAN ZADRA

PASS IT ON

A lost battle is a battle one thinks one has lost.

– FERDINAND FOCH

Life is a series of lessons that must be lived to be understood.

– RALPH WALDO EMERSON

I do not know the secret of success, but the key to failure is to try to please everyone.

– BILL COSBY

Obstacles cannot crush me; every obstacle yields stern resolve.

– LEONARDO DA VINCI

Our trials are tests; our sorrows pave the way for a fuller life when we have earned it.

– JEROME FLEISHMAN

When people do not make mistakes, I am uncomfortable. They are not reaching out and growing.

– FRANK RUCK

Are we willing to give up some things we like to do, in order to move on to those things we must do?

– SATENIG ST. MARIE

One who fears limits his activities. Failure is only the opportunity to more intelligently begin again.

– HENRY FORD

The tragedy of life is not that man loses but that he almost wins.

– HEYWOOD BROUN

Whatever comes, this too shall pass away
over time.

– ELLA WHEELER WILCOX

The past is but the beginning of a
beginning, and all that is and has been
is but the twilight of the dawn.

– H.G. WELLS

The greater the obstacle, the more glory
there is in overcoming it.

– MOLIERE

PASS IT ON

ANYONE WHO DARES

TO WASTE ONE HOUR OF LIFE

HAS NOT YET DISCOVERED

THE TRUE VALUE OF LIFE.

–CHARLES DARWIN

I tried and failed. I tried again
and succeeded.

– GAIL BORDEN, JR.

Those who do not know how to weep with
their whole heart do not know how to
laugh either.

– GOLDA MEIR

The greatest challenge of the day is:
how to bring about a revolution of the
heart, a revolution that has to start
with each one of us.

– DOROTHY DAY

PASS IT ON

The greatest test of courage on earth
is to bear defeat without losing heart.

– ROBERT GREEN INGERSOLL

You may have a fresh start any moment you
choose, for this thing that we call 'failure' is
not the falling down, but the staying down.

– MARY PICKFORD

In great attempts it is glorious even to fail.

– VINCE LOMBARDI

What matters is not the size of the dog in the fight, but the size of the fight in the dog.

– PAUL "BEAR" BRYANT

Unless you try to do something beyond what you have already mastered you will never grow.

– RONALD OSBORN

What is defeat? Nothing but education; nothing but the first step to something better.

– RICHARD SHERIDAN

Pursue perfection, but be willing to accept excellence.

— H. JACKSON BROWN, JR.

There is only one real failure in life that is possible, and that is not to be true to the best we know.

— FREDERICK FARRAR

The worst bankruptcy in the world is the person who has lost his enthusiasm.

— H.W. ARNOLD

If a man has talent and can't use it, he has failed. If he uses only half of it, he has partly failed. If he uses the whole of it, he has succeeded, and won a satisfaction and triumph few men ever know.

– THOMAS WOLFE

Success is not forever, and failure is not fatal.

– DON SHULA

The important thing is to learn a lesson every time you lose.

– JOHN MCENROE

No matter how much time you wasted
in the past, you still have an entire
tomorrow. Success depends upon using it
wisely by planning and setting priorities.

– DENNIS WAITLEY

There are two ways of meeting difficulties;
you alter the difficulties or you alter
yourself to meet them.

– PHYLLIS BOTTOME

What can you do to promote world peace?
Go home and love your family.

– MOTHER TERESA

When people are bored, it is primarily with
their own selves that they are bored.

– ERIC HOFFER

We are always getting ready to live,
but never living.

– RALPH WALDO EMERSON

Prosperity is not without many fears and
distaste; adversity not without many
comforts and hopes.

– FRANCIS BACON

There is but one success – to be able to spend your life in your own way.

– CHRISTOPHER MORLEY

The people who make a difference
are not the ones with the credentials,
but the ones with the concerns.

– MAX LUCADO

You can only lead others where you yourself
are willing to go.

– LACHLAN MCLEAN

What you think of yourself is much more important than what others think of you.

– SENECA

It takes no more time to see the good side of life than it takes to see the bad.

– JIMMY BUFFETT

The will to win is important, but the will to prepare is vital.

– JOE PATERNO

PASS IT ON

MY LIFE

IS MY MESSAGE.

–MAHATMA GANDHI

There is only one corner of the universe you can be certain of improving, and that is your own self.

– ALDOUS HUXLEY

It is a blessed thing that in every age someone has had enough individuality and courage to stand by his own convictions.

– ROBERT GREEN INGERSOLL

If you tell people the destination, but not how to get there, you'll be amazed at the results.

– GEORGE PATTON

Honesty is the first chapter in the book of wisdom.

– THOMAS JEFFERSON

Every individual has a place to fill in the world and is important in some respect, whether he chooses to be so or not.

– NATHANIEL HAWTHORNE

The team player knows that it doesn't matter who gets the credit as long as the job gets done. If the job gets done, the credit will come.

– THE EDGE

What you discover on your own is more exciting than what someone else discovers for you.

– DOUGLAS MACARTHUR

No one can give you better advice than yourself.

– MARCUS T. CICERO

Do what you can where you are with what you have been given.

– THEODORE ROOSEVELT

Knowing others is wisdom;
Knowing yourself is enlightenment;
Mastering others is strength;
Mastering yourself is true power.

– LAO-TZU

Patience means self-suffering.

– MAHATMA GANDHI

The final test of a gentleman is his respect
for those who can be of no possible value
to him.

– WILLIAM LYON PHELPS

It takes twenty years to build a reputation and five minutes to ruin it.

– JIMMY BUFFETT

Try not to become a man of success but rather try to become a man of value.

– ALBERT EINSTEIN

There are three things extremely hard – steel, a diamond, and to know one's self.

– BENJAMIN FRANKLIN

PASS IT ON

Chance happens to all, but to turn chance to account is the gift of few.

– ROBERT BULWER-LYTTON

We confide in our strength, without boasting of it; we respect that of others, without fearing it.

– THOMAS JEFFERSON

Education is not filling a bucket, but lighting a fire.

– WILLIAM YEATS

Most of my ideas belonged to other people who didn't bother to develop them.

– THOMAS EDISON

It is good to have money and the things that money can buy, but make sure you don't lose the things money can't buy through the process.

– GEORGE HORACE LORIMER

A positive attitude is like a fire; unless you continue to add fuel, it goes out.

– ALEXANDER LOCKHART

PASS IT ON

We each have a spark of life inside us, and we must set off that spark in one another.

– KENNY AUSUBEL

If we think about our own lives, we'll remember how much we learned from those who encouraged us.

– JOE NATHAN

Honesty is incompatible with amassing a large fortune.

– MAHATMA GANDHI

The most important single ingredient
in the formula of success is knowing
how to get along with people.

– THEODORE ROOSEVELT

The entire sum of existence is the magic
of being needed by just one person.

– VI PUTNAM

Men build too many walls and not
enough bridges.

– SIR ISAAC NEWTON

PASS IT ON

LIFE IS NOT ABOUT GETTING AHEAD

OF OTHER PEOPLE, BUT GETTING

AHEAD OF OURSELVES. TO BREAK

OUR OWN RECORD, TO OUTSTRIP

OUR YESTERDAYS BY TODAYS.

–PAUL C. BROWNLOW

There is a magnet in your heart that will attract true friends. That magnet is unselfishness and thinking of others first. When you learn to live for others, they will live for you.

– PARAMAHANSA YOGANANDA

My best friend is the one who brings out the best in me.

– HENRY FORD

Never contract a friendship with a man who is not better than yourself.

– CONFUCIUS

PASS IT ON

When you judge others, you are revealing your own fears and prejudices.

– H. JACKSON BROWN, JR.

No one can be the best at everything. But when all of us combine our talents, we can and will be the best at virtually anything.

– DAN ZADRA

At every stage of our lives, whatever is crowding out growth needs to be recognized and removed.

– JEAN SHINODA BOLEN

True friendship is like sound health; the value of it is seldom known until it is lost.

– CHARLES CALEB COLTON

One friend in a lifetime is much; two are many; three are hardly possible.

– HENRY BROOKS ADAMS

Each friend represents a world in us, a world possibly not born until they arrive, and it is only by this meeting that a new world is born.

– ANAIS NIN

PASS IT ON

A truly spiritual man's creed is not live and let live, but live and help live.

– ROGER BABSON

We are all in the same boat in a stormy sea, and we owe each other a terrible loyalty.

– G.K. CHESTERTON

It is a man's honor to avoid strife, but every fool is quick to quarrel.

– PROVERBS 20:3

The function of freedom is to free somebody else.

Never doubt that a small group of thoughtful, committed citizens can change the world; indeed, it is the only thing that ever has.

How good and pleasant it is when brothers dwell together in unity.

PASS IT ON

No matter what accomplishments you make, somebody helps you.

– ALTHEA GIBSON

Chains do not hold people together. It is the threads, the threads and textures of their values, which sew people together.

– CAMILLE CORDA LEE

There is little hope for us until we become tough minded enough to break loose from the shackles of prejudice, half-truths, and down-right ignorance.

– MARTIN LUTHER KING, JR.

We all take different paths in life, but no matter where we go, we take a little of each other everywhere.

– TIM MCGRAW

If we have a big enough 'why,' we will always discover the 'how.'

– TARA SEMISCH

Anger and intolerance are the twin enemies of correct understanding.

– MAHATMA GANDHI

Pass It On

Friendship without self-interest is one of the rare and beautiful things in life.

– JAMES BYRNES

Give me one friend, just one, who meets the needs of all my varying moods.

– ESTER CLARK

The first duty of love is to listen.

– PAUL TILLICH

He who sows courtesy reaps friendship and he who plants kindness gathers love.

– SAINT BASIL

Happiness is the delicate balance between what one is and what one has.

– F.H. DENISON

Our visions of a better future are real; dreams do come true; without that possibility, nature would not entice us to have them.

– JOHN UPDIKE

DON'T WALK IN FRONT OF ME,

I MAY NOT FOLLOW. DON'T WALK

BEHIND ME, I MAY NOT LEAD.

WALK BESIDE ME AND BE MY FRIEND.

–ALBERT CAMUS

Start right where you are. Distant fields always look greener, but opportunity lies right where you are. Take advantage of every opportunity of service.

– ROBERT COLLIER

Happiness is not a state to arrive at, but a manner of traveling.

– MARGARET LEE RUNBECK

Happiness resides not in possessions and not in gold; the feeling of happiness dwells in the soul.

– DEMOCRITUS

The secret of happiness is this: Let your interests be as wide as possible, and let your reactions to the things and persons that interest you be as far as possible friendly rather than hostile.

– BERTRAND RUSSELL

Very little is needed to make a happy life. It is all within yourself, in your way of thinking.

– MARCUS AURELIUS

To love is to place our happiness in the happiness of another.

– G.W. VON LEIBNITZ

The moments of happiness we enjoy take us by surprise. It is not that we seize them, but that they seize us.

– ASHLEY MONTAGU

Whoever is happy will make others happy too. He who has courage and faith will never perish in misery.

– ANNE FRANK

Happiness lies in the joy of achievement and the thrill of creative effort.

– FRANKLIN D. ROOSEVELT

PASS IT ON

Let us begin to see the true promise of our country and community, not as a melting pot, but as a kaleidoscope.

– ROBERT KENNEDY

We all live under the same sky, but we don't have the same horizon.

– KONRAD ADENAUER

The future belongs to those who believe in the beauty of their dreams.

– BENJAMIN DISRAELI

Real generosity is doing something nice
for someone who'll never find it out.

– FRANK CLARK

The secret of a happy life is to accept
change gracefully.

– JAMES STEWART

Go there together! Imagination is the
fabulous country – the place where miracles
not only happen, but where they happen
all the time.

– THOMAS WOLFE

PASS IT ON

Most people are about as happy as they make up their minds to be.

– ABRAHAM LINCOLN

Always be a little kinder than necessary.

– JAMES BARRIE

I am determined to be cheerful and happy in whatever situation I may be; For I have also learned from experience that the greater part of our happiness or misery depends upon our disposition, and not upon our circumstances.

– MARTHA WASHINGTON

Man needs, for his happiness, not only the enjoyment of this and that, but hope and enterprise and change.

– BERTRAND RUSSELL

Keep your face to the sunshine and you can't see the shadow.

– HELEN KELLER

To live in society doesn't mean simply living side by side with others in a more or less close cohesion; it means living through one another and for one another.

– PAUL-EUGEME RAY

A man should never be ashamed to own that he has been in the wrong, which is but saying that he is wiser today than he was yesterday.

– ALEXANDER POPE

Our country is not made up of stocks or bonds or gold – it is comprised of the hopes and dreams in our minds and hearts.

– BENJAMIN HARRISON

What wisdom can you find that is greater than kindness?

– JEAN JACQUES ROUSSEAU

No natural boundary seems to be set to the efforts of man, and in his eyes, what is not yet done is only what he has not yet attempted to do.

– ALEXIS DE TOCQUEVILLE

Half the world is composed of people who have something to say and can't, while the other half who have nothing to say just keep on saying it.

– ROBERT FROST

He is happiest, be king or peasant, who finds peace in his home.

– JOHANN WOLFGANG VON GOETHE

IT TAKES LIFE

TO LOVE LIFE.

–EDGAR LEE MASTERS

When one door of happiness closes, another opens. Often though, we look so long at the closed door that we do not see the one which has been opened for us.

– HELEN KELLER

We were not sent into this world to do anything into which we cannot put our heart.

– JOHN RUSKIN

Whatever comes from the heart carries the heat and color of its birthplace.

– OLIVER WENDELL HOLMES, SR.

Make each day useful and cheerful and prove that you know the worth of time by employing it well. Then youth will be happy, old age without regret and life a beautiful success.

– LOUISA MAY ALCOTT

I have learned to seek my happiness by limiting my desires, rather than in attempting to satisfy them.

– JOHN STUART MILL

People see only what they are prepared to see.

– RALPH WALDO EMERSON

When you were born you cried and the world rejoiced. Live your life in such a manner that when you die the world cries and you rejoice.

– ANCIENT SAYING FROM INDIA

The U.S. Constitution doesn't guarantee happiness, only the pursuit of it. You have to catch up with it yourself.

– BENJAMIN FRANKLIN

I never pray that I may win. I just ask for the courage to do my very best.

– GARY PLAYER

Happiness always looks small while you hold it in your hands, but let it go and you learn at once how big and precious it is.

— MAXIM GORKY

What lies behind us and what lies before us are tiny matters compared to what lies within us.

— RALPH WALDO EMERSON

If you are lucky enough to find a way of life you love, you have to find the courage to live it.

— JOHN IRVING

You will find, as you look back upon your life, that the moments when you really lived are the moments when you have done things in the spirit of love.

– HENRY DRUMMOND

You are forgiven for your happiness and your successes only if you generously consent to share them.

– ALBERT CAMUS

The greatest lesson in life is to know that even fools are right sometimes.

– WINSTON CHURCHILL

It is not enough to be busy. The question is, "What are we busy about?"

Leadership is the art of getting someone else to do something you want done because he wants to do it.

It is not the employer who pays wages; he only handles the money. It is the product that pays wages.

Never tell people how to do things.
Tell them what to do and they will
surprise you with their integrity.

– GEORGE PATTON

Silence is the ultimate weapon of power.

– CHARLES DE GAULLE

The best executive is the one who has
sense enough to pick good men to do
what he wants done, and self-restraint
enough to keep from meddling
with them while they do it.

– THEODORE ROOSEVELT

PASS IT ON

A leader's role is to raise people's aspirations for what they can become and to release their energies so they will try to get there.

– DAVID GERGEN

Excellence is to do a common thing in an uncommon way.

– BOOKER T. WASHINGTON

In the moment of decision, the best thing you can do is the right thing to do. The worst thing you can do is nothing.

– THEODORE ROOSEVELT

The price of greatness is responsibility.

– WINSTON CHURCHILL

I find that the greatest thing in this world is not so much where we stand, as in what direction we are moving.

– OLIVER WENDELL HOLMES, SR.

Leadership is the courage to admit mistakes, the vision to welcome change, the enthusiasm to motivate others, and the confidence to stay out of step when everyone else is marching to the wrong tune.

– E.M. ESTES

PASS IT ON

I NEVER DID ANYTHING WORTH

DOING BY ACCIDENT, NOR DID

ANY OF MY INVENTIONS COME BY

ACCIDENT, THEY CAME BY WORK.

–THOMAS EDISON

We are what we consistently do.
Excellence, therefore, is not an act
but a habit.

– ARISTOTLE

Conviction is worthless unless it is
converted into conduct.

– THOMAS CARLYLE

What makes leadership is the ability to get
people to do what they don't want to do,
and make them like it.

– HARRY TRUMAN

PASS IT ON

Few will have the greatness to bend history itself; but each of us can work to change a small portion of events, and in the total of all those acts will be written the history of this generation.

– ROBERT KENNEDY

It is not by whining that one carries out the job of a leader.

– NAPOLEON BONAPARTE

Half-heartedness never won a battle.

– WILLIAM MCKINLEY

Let us realize that the privilege to work is a gift, the power to work is a blessing, the love of work is success.

– DAVID O. MCKAY

The only ones among you who will be really happy are those who will have sought and found how to serve.

– ALBERT SCHWEITZER

Character is developed by what we repeatedly do rather than by what we repeatedly say.

– CARL BARBER STEELE

PASS IT ON

The world is divided into people who do things and people who get the credit; try to belong to the first class – there's far less competition.

– DWIGHT WHITNEY MORROW

Nothing is so potent as the silent influence of a good example.

– JAMES KENT

If you don't back it up with performance and hard work, talking doesn't mean a thing.

– MICHAEL JORDAN

Education should prepare people not just
to earn a living but to live a life –
a creative, humane and sensitive life.

– CHARLES SILBERMAN

The difference between failure and success
is doing a thing nearly right and doing a
thing exactly right.

– EDWARD SIMMONS

A total commitment is paramount to
reaching the ultimate in performance.

– TOM FLORES

PASS IT ON

The way a team plays as a whole determines its success. You may have the greatest bunch of individual stars in the world, but if they don't play together, the club won't be worth a dime.

– BABE RUTH

He who has confidence in himself will lead the rest.

– HORACE

Winners have simply formed the habit of doing things losers don't like to do.

– ALBERT GRAY

The great organizations celebrate the differences. They seek harmony, not uniformity. They hire talent, not color. They strive for oneness, not sameness.

– GIL ATKINSON

Ambition is an idol on whose wings great minds are carried only to extreme; to be sublimely great or to be nothing.

– ROBERT SOUTHEY

Make yourself necessary to somebody.

– RALPH WALDO EMERSON

PASS IT ON

A single thought in the morning may fill our whole day with joy and sunshine or gloom and depression.

Worry doesn't empty tomorrow of its sorrow; it empties today of its strength.

If I can count on you, and you can count on me, just think what a wonderful world this will be.

Anyone can hold the helm when the sea is calm. Strength is proven in adversity.

– PUBLIUS SYRUS

The greatest discovery of my generation is that human beings, by changing the inner attitudes of their minds, can change the outer aspects of their lives.

– WILLIAM JAMES

All change is not growth; all movements not forward.

– ELLEN GLASGOW

A GREAT MAN SHOWS

HIS GREATNESS BY THE WAY

HE TREATS LITTLE MEN.

–THOMAS CARLYLE

You don't raise heroes; you raise sons.
And if you treat them like sons, they'll turn
out to be heroes, even if it's just in your
own eyes.

– WALTER SCHIRRA, SR.

When it comes to winning, you need the
skill and the will.

– FRANK TYGER

Our hearts, our hopes, our prayers, our
tears, our faith triumphant o'er our fears,
are all with thee.

– HENRY WADSWORTH LONGFELLOW

The only disability in life is a bad attitude.

– SCOTT HAMILTON

One person with a belief is equal to a force of ninety-nine who have only interests.

– JOHN STUART MILL

We will compromise on almost anything, but not on our values, or our aesthetics, or our idealism, or our sense of curiosity.

– ANITA RODDICK

The journey is the true reward.

– OLD SAYING

Every great and commanding movement
in the annals of the world is the triumph
of enthusiasm. Nothing great was ever
achieved without it.

– RALPH WALDO EMERSON

Believe that life is worth living, and
your belief will help create the fact.

– WILLIAM JAMES

I am delighted that even at my great age
ideas come to me, the pursuit of which
would require another lifetime.

– JOHANN WOLFGANG VON GOETHE

What does not kill you will make
you stronger.

– FRIEDRICH NIETZSCHE

Excellence is never an accident.

– H. JACKSON BROWN, JR.

It is hard to beat a person who never gives up.

– BABE RUTH

The future belongs to those who prepare for it.

– RALPH WALDO EMERSON

A great man is a man who lives great principles. The greatest men the world has ever known were criticized, often bitterly, but they did not let themselves get discouraged. This is one of the secrets of their greatness.

– STRENGTH FOR A MAN'S HEART

PASS IT ON

We have not inherited the earth from our fathers, we are borrowing it from our children.

God did not write solo parts for very many of us. He expects us to be participants in the great symphony of life.

Seeking diversity automatically leads us to excellence, just as focusing on excellence inevitably leads us to diversity.

Nothing can stop the man with the right mental attitude from achieving his goal; nothing on earth can help the man with the wrong mental attitude.

– THOMAS JEFFERSON

Light tomorrow with today.

– ELIZABETH BARRETT BROWNING

Optimism doesn't wait on facts. It deals with prospects. Pessimism is a waste of time.

– NORMAN COUSINS

PASS IT ON

Never hesitate to hold out your hand,
never hesitate to accept the outstretched
hand of another.

– POPE JOHN XXII

We cannot tell what may happen to us
in the strange medley of life. But we can
decide what happens in us. How we take it,
what we do with it, and that is what really
counts in the end.

– JOSEPH F. NEWTON

If you aren't fired with enthusiasm,
you will be fired with enthusiasm.

– VINCE LOMBARDI

If you don't invest very much, then defeat doesn't hurt very much and winning is not very exciting.

– DICK VERMEIL

The most important thing I have learned is the difference between taking one's work seriously and taking one's self seriously.

– MARGARET FONTEY

A positive mind has extra solving power.

– ALEXANDER LOCKHART

PASS IT ON

IT'S NOT WHETHER

YOU GET KNOCKED DOWN,

IT'S WHETHER YOU GET UP.

–VINCE LOMBARDI

Life's battles don't always go to the stronger or faster man; but sooner or later, the man who wins is the one who thinks he can.

– C.W. LONGENECKER

I believe in discipline. You can forgive incompetence. You can forgive lack of ability. But one thing you cannot ever forgive is the lack of discipline.

– FOREST GREGG

Let us not look back in anger, nor forward in fear, but around in awareness.

– JAMES THURBER

Only by taking risks, which means the discovery of dead-ends, do we achieve real breakthroughs.

– RICHARD SENNETT

When you get into a tight place and everything goes against you till it seems as though you could not hold on one minute longer, never give up then, for that is just the place and time that the tide will turn.

– HARRIET BEECHER STOWE

Well done is better than well said.

– BENJAMIN FRANKLIN

Love lives on hope, and dies when hope is dead; it is a flame which sinks for lack of fuel.

– PIERRE CORNEILLE

The best way to cope with change is to help create it.

– ROBERT DOLE

Confidence comes not from always being right but not fearing to be wrong.

– PETER T. MCINTYRE

I have always believed I could help change the world, because I have been lucky to have adults around me who actually did.

– MARIAN WRIGHT EDELMAN

Everything should be made as simple as possible, but not simpler.

– ALBERT EINSTEIN

It is hard to fail; but it is worse never to have tried to succeed.

– THEODORE ROOSEVELT

You can gain strength, courage and confidence by every experience in which you really stop to look fear in the face. You must do the thing which you think you cannot do.

– ELEANOR ROOSEVELT

One man with courage makes a majority.

– ANDREW JACKSON

The high wage begins down in the shop. If it is not created there it cannot get into pay envelopes. There will never be a system invented which will do away with necessity for work.

– HENRY FORD

PASS IT ON

I would rather live in a world where my life is surrounded by mystery than live in a world so small that my mind could comprehend it.

— HENRY EMERSON FOSDICK

But above all, try something.

— FRANKLIN D. ROOSEVELT

Nothing great will ever be achieved without great men, and great men are great only if they are determined to be.

— CHARLES DE GAULLE

The quality of a person's life is in direct proportion to their commitment to excellence, regardless of their chosen field of endeavor.

– VINCE LOMBARDI

Eighty percent of success is simply showing up.

– WOODY ALLEN

The energy, the faith, the devotion which we bring to this endeavor will light our country and all who serve it, and the glow from that fire can truly light the world.

– JOHN F. KENNEDY

PASS IT ON

A SHIP IN HARBOR IS SAFE,

BUT THAT IS NOT WHAT

SHIPS ARE BUILT FOR.

–JOHN SHEDD

If a man is called to be a streetsweeper, he should sweep streets even as Michelangelo painted, or Beethoven composed music, or Shakespeare wrote poetry. He should sweep streets so well that all the hosts of heaven and earth will pause to say, here lived a great streetsweeper who did his job well.

– MARTIN LUTHER KING, JR.

Every man dies, but not every man lives.

– WILLIAM WALLACE

Fear not that thy life shall come to an end, but rather fear that it shall never have a beginning.

– JOHN HENRY NEWMAN

Pass It On

Trust each other again and again.
When the trust level gets high enough,
people transcend apparent limitations and
discover new and awesome abilities that
were previously unapparent.

– DAVID ARMISTEAD

The world and its desires pass away,
but the man who does the will of God
lives forever.

– 1 JOHN 2:17

We can do no great things; only small
things with great love.

– MOTHER TERESA

A hero is no braver than an ordinary man, but he is braver five minutes longer.

– RALPH WALDO EMERSON

The real contest is always between what you've done and what you're capable of doing. You measure yourself against yourself and nobody else.

– GEOFFREY GABERING

Always do right. This will gratify some people and astonish the rest.

– MARK TWAIN

PASS IT ON

What kind of man would live where there is no daring? I don't believe in taking foolish chances, but nothing can be accomplished without taking any chance at all.

– CHARLES LINDBERGH

The secret of success in life is for man to be ready for his opportunity when it comes.

– BENJAMIN DISRAELI

A great pleasure in life is doing what people say you cannot do.

– WALTER GAGEHOT

Use what talents you have; the woods
would have little music if no birds sang
their song except those who sang best.

– OLIVER G. WILSON

Courage is the power to let go
of the familiar.

– RAYMOND LINGUIST

You don't concentrate on risks.
You concentrate on results. No risk is
too great to prevent the necessary job
from getting done.

– CHUCK YEAGER

PASS IT ON

To avoid criticism… do nothing…
say nothing… be nothing.

– ELBERT HUBBARD

A positive thinker does not refuse to
recognize the negative; he refuses to dwell
on it.

– ALEXANDER LOCKHART

No trumpets sound when the important
decisions of our life are made. Destiny is
made known silently.

– AGNES DE MILLE

We must free ourselves of the hope that the sea will ever rest. We must learn to sail in high winds.

– HANMER PARSONS GRANT

Ideas are poor ghosts until they become incarnate in a person. Then they look out through eyes of compassion. Then they touch with redemptive hands... and shake the world like a passion.

– GEORGE ELIOT

Success is not how far you get in life, but how far you go from where you started. Success goes to fighters, not quitters.

– M. KAY DUPONT

PASS IT ON

I am only one, but I am one. I cannot do everything but I can do something. What I can do I ought to do. And what I ought to do I will do, by the grace of God to the best of my ability.

– EDWARD EVERETT HALE

I have found enthusiasm for work to be the most priceless ingredient in any recipe for success.

– SAMUEL GOLDWYN

Decide what you want, decide what you are willing to exchange for it. Establish your priorities and go to work.

– H.L. HUNT

There are many things in life that will catch your eye, but only a few will catch your heart. Pursue these.

– MICHAEL NOLAN

We've removed the ceiling above our dreams. There are no more impossible dreams.

– JESSE JACKSON

The key is to keep company with people who uplift you, whose presence calls forth your best.

– ELIZABETH WILLETT

Be careful, think about the effect of what you say. Your words should be constructive, bring people together, not apart.

– MIRIAM MAKEBA

If you are not guided by God, you will be guided by someone or something else.

– ERIC LIDDELL

To make a difference is not a matter of accident, a matter of casual occurrence of the tides. People choose to make a difference.

– MAYA ANGELOU

You've got to create a dream. You've got to uphold the dream. If you can't, go back to the factory or go back to the desk.

– ERIC BURDON

Because where we come from isn't nearly as important as where we are going.

– FARESTART

Life is a great big canvas, and you should throw all the paint on it you can.

– DANNY KAYE

Additional Copies

If interested in additional copies of *Pass It On*, they may be
ordered directly from Vital Communications Motivation, Inc.,
at (501) 868-8195 or online at www.paulvitale.com.

Also by Paul Vitale

Are You Puzzled by the Puzzle of Life?
Lessons to Remember as You Pursue Your Purpose

Are You Puzzled by the Puzzle of Life? Teacher's Guide
A One-Step Guide for the Classroom

Seminars and Presentations

For additional information on Paul Vitale's seminars and
presentations, please contact Vital Communications
Motivation, Inc., at www.paulvitale.com.